Birthplace of Will Rogers near Claremore, Oklahoma.

Will Rogers

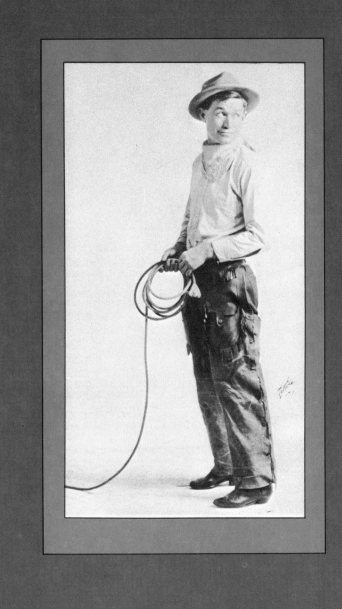

Will Rogers

Wise and Witty Sayings
of A Great American Humorist
Selected by Art Wortman
With Photographs
From the Collection
of the Will Rogers Memorial,
Claremore, Oklahoma

HALLMARK EDITIONS

Set at The Castle Press in Trump Medieval,
A Venetian typeface designed by
Professor Georg Trump, Munich.
Printed on Hallmark Eggshell Book paper.
Designed by William Gilmore.
Library of Congress Catalog Card Number: 76-102168.
Standard Book Number: 87529-026-4.

I remember my father with reverence and laughter. To many he was an Oklahoma cowboy, with a hair lick over his forehead, an infectious grin, twirling a long lariat, and speaking a language of his own that bit big chunks into the sham of his day. He's thought of as a humorist. He was, but he was more, too. He was never an actor, though his name blazed in lights from Hollywood and Broadway to Berlin and Alaska.

Will Rogers had an attitude toward humor different from most of the humorists of today.

To begin with, he wrote all of his own material. When a Hollywood gag-man offered to write jokes for him for a thousand dollars a week, Will Rogers replied, "For a thousand dollars a week, I'll write jokes for you." And he could have, too.

Secondly, he said that he wanted his humor to make a point, to say something true. At the time of the first world war he wrote, "We don't have secret diplomacy. American diplomacy is an open book—generally a checkbook." Not a big laugh, but it points up a condition that is still true today.

Finally, and I think most important, there was no malice to his humor. He never criticized a man who was down. He was neither a Republican nor a Democrat. He said he was always with the 'outs' and against the 'ins.' At the start of the great depression, Will Rogers ceased all criticisms of the President. "Let's stop blaming the President and the Republicans for all this," he wrote. "Why, they're not smart enough to have thought of all that's been happening to us lately."

He had a sharp wit, but he used it kindly. In his daily column, which appeared on the morning front page of nearly 400 newspapers, he took cracks at capital and labor, bankers and farmers, but through it all there was the thread of forgiveness and national unity. The insulting, personal humor of today was quite foreign to Will Rogers.

He lived in a time that is now long past, when more people lived in the country than the city. I think his point of view is best summed up in a remark he once made to an audience in New York, "They may call me a 'rube' and a 'hick,' but I'd a lot rather be the man who bought the Brooklyn Bridge than the man who sold it." That was Will Rogers.

Will Rogers

This country is not where it is today on account of any one man. It is here on account of the real common sense of the Big Normal Majority.

If you can start arguing over something, and get enough publicity, and keep the argument going, you can divide our nation overnight as to whether spinach or broccoli are the most nutritious.

We can get hot and bothered quicker over nothing, and cool off faster than any nation in the world.

The way we do things, always have done things and always will do things, there just has to be so much graft. We wouldn't feel good if there wasn't. We just have to get used to charging so much off to graft just like you charge off so much for insurance, taxes or depreciation.

Russians I don't think would ever be as happy as we are . . . for they haven't got as much to laugh at as we have here. Perhaps we're not the most humorous people in the world, but the provocations to humor is greater in this country than anywhere else in the world. There's not a minute that there's not some of us doing something seriously that brings smiles to everybody else over here.

America invents everything, but the trouble is we get tired of it the minute the new is wore off.

Male and Female

Money and women are the most sought after and the least known about of any two things we have.

If you let [women] have their way, you will generally get even with them in the end.

The two finest things that can happen to a man is to have a good wife and to know that he's accepted by the people he comes from.

In parts of India they have a law that if a man is married and is unfaithful to his wife, her family can take him out and publicly shoot him. There is no trial or anything. It is just their religious

8

and state custom (and we call them uncivilized).
Well, anyway, if that was the custom over here,
I would take every cent I make and put it into
an ammunition factory.

There is nothing as determined as a woman that
carries on, and there is millions of 'em.

You can't pass a park without seeing a statue of
some old codger on a horse, it must be his brav-
ery, you can tell it isn't his horsemanship. Wom-
en are twice as brave as men, yet they never
seem to have reached the statue stage.

On "Civilization"

There ain't no civilization where there ain't no
satisfaction and that's what's the trouble now.
Nobody is satisfied.

That's one trouble with our charities, we are always saving somebody away off, when the fellow next to us ain't eating. Something wrong
with the missionaries. They will save anybody
if he is far enough away and don't speak our
language.

Something ought to be done about these "primitive" people who live in various parts of the world, and don't know a thing but to live off what nature provides. You would think they would get civilized and learn to live off each other like us civilized folks do.

I doubt very much if civilization (so called) has helped generosity. I bet the old cave man would divide his raw meat with you as quick as one of us will ask a down-and-out to go in and have a meal with us. . . . Civilization hasn't done much but make you wash your teeth, and in those days gnawing on bones and meat made tooth paste unnecessary.

The Pace of Life

This is an age of progress. Live fast and die quick. The human side of anything can't compare with so-called progress.

I have never yet seen a man in such a big hurry that a horse or train wouldn't have got him there in plenty of time. In fact, nine-tenths of the people would be better off if they stayed where they are, instead of going where they are going. No man in America if he didn't get where he is going would be missed.

People take themselves too serious. They think if they don't break their neck from one place of business to another then the world will stop. Say, all they have to do is just watch some man die that is more prominent than they are, and in less than twenty-four hours the world has forgot he ever lived; so they ought to have imagination enough to know how long they will stop things if they left this old earth. People nowadays are traveling faster, but they are not getting any further (in fact not as far) as our old dads did.

Prosperity American Style

I have been in many a country . . . and they have thousands of problems. But America's problem as to "where to invest my money?" is unique. The whole world would give their right leg to be bothered with that problem.

We are a people that get tired of a thing awful quick and I believe this continual prosperity will begin to get monotonous with us. We can't go through life just eating cake all the time. Of course, we like prosperity but we are having so much of it that we just can't afford it.

No nation in the history of the world was ever sitting as pretty. If we want anything, all we have to do is go and buy it on credit.

So that leaves us without any economic problems whatsoever, except perhaps some day to have to pay for them.

We'll show the world we are prosperous, even if we have to go broke to do it.

We will never get anywhere with our finances till we pass a law saying that every time we appropriate something we got to pass another bill along with it stating where the money is coming from.

Taxes and Finance

Alexander Hamilton originated the "put and take" system into our national treasury. The tax payers put it in and the politicians take it out.

Congress knocked the rich in the creek with a seventy-two per cent income tax. Then somebody must have told 'em, "Yes, Congress, you got 'em while they are living, but what if they die on you to keep from paying it?"

Congress says, "Well, never thought of that, so we will frame one that will get 'em, alive or living, dead or deceased."

Now they got such a high inheritance tax on 'em that you won't catch these old rich boys dying promiscuously like they did. This bill makes patriots out of everybody. You sure do die for your country, if you die from now on.

Taxation is about all there is to government. People don't want their taxes lowered near as much as the politician tries to make you believe. People want *just* taxes more than they want *lower* taxes. They want to know that every man is paying his proportionate share according to his wealth.

I don't see why a man shouldn't pay inheritance tax. If a country is good enough to pay taxes to while you are living, it's good enough to pay in after you die. By the time you die, you should be so used to paying taxes that it would almost be second nature anyway.

The big yell comes nowadays from the taxpayers. But I guess when the Pilgrims landed on Plymouth Rock and they had the whole of the American continent, and all they had to do to get an extra 160 acres was to shoot another Indian, I bet you anything they kicked on the price of ammunition. I bet they said, "What's this country coming to that we have to spend a nickle for powder?" Of course, they got the lead back after they dissected the Indian. No matter what you pay for taxes, high, low or medium, the yell is always the same, 100 per cent.

The income tax has made more liars out of the American people than golf has. Even when you make [a tax form] out on the level, you don't know when it's through if you are a crook or a martyr.

The High Cost of Living

Got a wire today from an old boy in Parsons, Kansas, and he wanted me to enter in a hog-calling contest; you know I used to be an awful good hog caller when hogs were cheap, but the way hogs have gone up in price it's changed the

whole system of calling 'em. It would take Henry Ford hollering with his check book to get one to come to you nowadays. I hollered all morning just for three slices of bacon and it didn't come, so there ain't much use of me howling my head off to try and get a whole hog to come.

Last year we said, "Things can't go on like this," and they didn't, they got worse.

Let advertisers spend the same amount of money improving their product that they do on advertising and they wouldn't have to advertise it.

Did you see the figures issued by the Department of Commerce about the amount men spent on cosmetics to beautify themselves? Didn't I tell you they are getting vainer over their looks than women?

They spent over $1,000,000,000 and there is more bald-headed ones and more ugly ones and more funny-looking ones than we ever had before. They will try anything in the world a woman does. They will have dresses on in less than ten years.

Our problem is not what is the dollar worth in London, Rome, or Paris, or what even it is worth at home. It's how to get hold of it, whatever it's worth!

The Prohibition Era

Will said that he did not feel strongly one way or the other about Prohibition, but on the whole he tended to oppose it as unwise. "If we must sin," he quipped, "let's sin quick and don't let it be a long, lingering sinning."

The only way you could tell a citizen from a bootlegger in Kansas was the bootlegger would be sober.

I see where [the Prohibitionists] now propose to stop cigarettes first and then profanity. They are going to have a rough time with that profanity, cause as long as there is a prohibitionist living there will be profanity!

Why don't they pass a Constitutional Amendment prohibiting anybody from learning anything? And if it works as good as the Prohibition one did, in five years we would have the smartest race of people on earth.

Somebody figured out now that we can have two and three quarter per cent beer. But who wants to drink thirty-seven and-a-half bottles to be 100 per cent drunk?

The prohibitionists rave about water. Now Noah knew more about water than all of them put together. He was the water commissioner of his time. He was an expert on water and the first man smart enough *not* to drink it.

He was the first one to discover a use for it, that was to float a boat on, but as a beverage he knew it was a total failure.

The wine had such ill effects on Noah's health that it was all he could do to live 950 years. Just nineteen years short of Methusaleh. . . . Show me a total abstainer that ever lived that long!

Well, Prohibition is better than no liquor at all.

These reformers are always wanting to save you; and if it wasn't for them, people wouldn't need saving.

Personally I think the saloon men put this prohibition through, as they have sold more in the last year than in any ten previous years before.

If you think this country ain't dry, watch 'em vote; if you think this country ain't wet, watch 'em drink. They will vote dry as long as they can stagger to the polls.

If they could take people's breath instead of their vote you would get the true sentiment of the country.

On Crime and The Courts

It looks like after a person's guilt in this country is established, why then the battle as to whether he should be punished is the real test of the court. Of course if a fellow is never convicted and never confesses, why then they will hang him. But if he is lucky enough to get convicted or confess he has a great chance of coming clear.

There is two types of larceny, petty and grand, and the courts will really give you a longer sentence for petty than they do for grand. They are supposed to be the same in the eyes of the law, but the judges always put a little extra on for petty, as a kind of a fine for stupidness. "If that's all you got you ought to go to jail longer."

Will in a scene from *The Hanging Fool*.

Another innocent bystander shot in New York yesterday. You just stand around this town long enough and be innocent and somebody is going to shoot you. One day they shot four. That's the best shooting ever done in this town. Any time you can find four innocent people in New York in one day you are doing well even if you don't shoot 'em.

The Art of Politics

We have been staggering along now about 155 years under every conceivable horse thief that could get into office, and yet here we are, still going strong.

I doubt if Barnum's Circus, or Hagenbeck's Wild Animal Show have housed as many different kinds of species as has been in our Government employ during its existence. Yet as bad as they are they can't spoil it, and as good as they are they can't help it. . . .

A good man can't do nothing in office because the System is against him, and a bad one can't do anything for the same reason. So bad as we are, we are better off than any other nation, so what's the use to worry?

Slogan: "Be a politician; no training necessary."

No one is going to spoil the country but the people. No one man can do it and all the people are not going to do it, so it's going to run in spite of all the mistakes that can happen to it.

Common sense is not an issue in politics; it's an affliction.

Neither is honesty an issue in politics. It's a miracle. . . .

I keep saying I'm a Democrat, but I ain't. I just pretend to be 'cause Democrats are funny and I'm supposed to be.

On National Conventions

If we didn't have two parties, we would all settle on the best men in the country and things would run fine. But as it is, we settle on the worst ones and then fight over 'em.

If you eliminate the names of Lincoln, Washington, Roosevelt, Jackson and Wilson, both parties' political conventions would get out three days earlier.

The Republican Convention [1928] opened with a prayer. If the Lord can see his way clear to bless the Republican Party the way it's been carrying on, then the rest of us ought to get it without even asking for it.

Simeon D. Fess delivered what is called the Keynote Speech. A Keynote Speech is press notices of the Republican Party written by its own members.

Here are just a few of the things that I bet you didn't know the Republicans were responsible for: radio, telephones, baths, automobiles, savings accounts, enforcement, workmen living in houses, and a living wage for Senators.

Always excitement at a Democratic anything! There is always something that will stir up an argument even if they all agree.

At a Democratic National Convention, Will wrote: Ah! They was Democrats today, and we was proud of 'em. They fought, they fit, they split, and adjourned in a dandy wave of dissension. That's the old Democratic spirit. A whole day wasted and nothing done. I tell you, they are getting back to normal. . . .

The Democrats had brought on war, pestilence, debts, disease, boll weevil, gold teeth, need of farm relief, suspenders, floods, famines.

He told of so much money that we had saved that I think if he had talked another hour he would have paid us a dividend.

It was an impromptu address that he had been working on for only six months.

He made no attempt to oratory, he just shouted.

A Democrat never adjourns. He is born, becomes of voting age and starts right in arguing over something, and his political adjournment is his date with the undertaker. Politics is business with the Democrat. He don't work at it, but he tells what he would do if he was working at it.

Political dealing makes Presidents, more than ability, but as bad as we are, and as funny as we do things, we are better off than the other countries, so bring on more conventions. No nation likes "hooey" like we do. We are all cuckoo, but we are happy.

Still, a politician is not as narrow-minded as he forces himself to be.

Elections and Parties

If a man could tell the difference between the two parties he would make a sucker out of Solomon for wisdom. This country runs in spite of parties; in fact parties are the biggest handicaps we have to contend with. If we didn't have to stop to play politics, any administration could almost make a Garden of Eden out of us.

The short memories of American voters is what keeps our politicians in office.

Wouldn't it be great if [other countries] started electing by the ballot instead of by the bullet, and us electing by the ballot instead of by the bullion?

Just finished shooting scenes here in Washington for a movie of the old stage play *A Texas Steer*. It was the story of a man elected to Washington on bought votes. We are bringing it up to date by not changing it at all. . . .

The Republicans have a habit of having three bad years and one good one, and the good one always happens to be election year.

I would rather have two friends in the counting room than a Republican slush fund behind me. More candidates have been defeated after six o'clock in the evening than were ever defeated during election day.

Political elections . . . are a good deal like marriages, there's no accounting for anyone's taste.

Papers today say, "What would Lincoln do today?" Well, in the first place, he wouldn't chop any wood, he would trade his ax in on a Ford. Being a Republican he would vote the Democratic ticket. Being in sympathy for the underdog he would be classed as a radical progressive. Having a sense of humor he would be called eccentric.

When a party can't think of anything else they always fall back on lower taxes, but no voter has lived to see the day when his taxes were lowered. Presidents have been promising lower taxes since Washington crossed the Delaware by hand in a row boat, but our taxes have gotten bigger

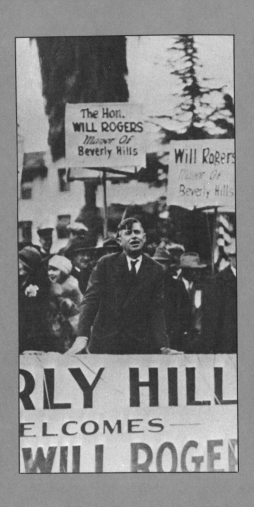

and their boats have gotten larger until now the President crosses the Delaware in his private yacht.

I was born on Election Day, but never was able to get elected to anything. I am going to jump out some day and be indefinite enough about everything that they will call me a politician, then run on a platform of question marks, and be elected unanimously, then reach in the treasury and bring back my district a new bridge, or tunnel, or dam, and I will be a statesman.

Some of our Presidents

George Washington was a surveyor. He took the exact measure of the British and surveyed himself out about the most valuable piece of land in America at that time, Mount Vernon. George could not only tell the truth but land values.

Andrew Jackson was the first one to think up the idea to promise everybody that if they will vote for you, you will give them an office when you get it, and the more times they vote for you, the bigger the office.

Every politician talks about Lincoln, but none of them ever imitate him.

President Taft, what a lovely old soul. Fat and good natured. . . . He always seemed like he was one of us. He was our great human fellow because there was more of him to be human.

I told [President Harding] I wanted to tell him all the latest political jokes. He said, "I know 'em, I appointed most of them."
　　So I saw I couldn't match humor with this man, so I called it a day.

Once a friend bet Will that he couldn't make President Coolidge laugh. But Will won. When he was introduced to Coolidge, he said: Beg pardon, I didn't catch the name.

[President Coolidge] kept his mouth shut. That was such a novelty among politicians, that it just swept the country. Originality will be rewarded in any line.

Here comes Coolidge and does nothing and retires a hero, not only because he hadn't done anything, but because he had done it better than anyone.

I always did want to see [Herbert Hoover] elected. I wanted to see how far a competent man could go in politics. It has never been tried before.

There has been many who has had to say, "Mister, can you spare a dime," but President Roosevelt is the first man in the history of the world who looked a nation right in the face and said, "Mister, can you spare ten billion dollars?" Well, Congress and the American people considered it such a compliment to be asked for that much that they really liked it.

President [Franklin D.] Roosevelt . . . held up for his Brain Trust. He said he would take brains anytime in preference to politics. He just as good as admitted you couldn't get both in the same body.

I am down in Old Virginia, the mother of Presidents when we thought Presidents had to be aristocrats. Since we got wise to the limitations of aristocrats, Virginia has featured their ham over their Presidential timber.

You hear people say, "What is this New Deal, anyhow?" Well, there was a headline today that explains it. "Wall Street anxiously awaits the President's message." In the "old deal," it was the President that was anxiously awaiting till Wall Street sent *him* the message to read.

You can always joke good-naturedly a big man, but be sure he is a big man before you joke about him.

On Congress

Legislatures are . . . like animals in a zoo. You can't do anything about 'em. All you can do is just stand and watch 'em.

I asked [Vice-President], Garner, who drank more, House or Senate? "Well," he said, "It's almost a tie, but I believe the House drinks more, not much, but a little more. You see there is 531 in there and only 96 in the Senate. If the Senate had about two more members they would go ahead of 'em."

Take it all in all, I believe [Congress] ought to have their raise. We are a rich nation and our officials should be the best paid in the world.

The principal bad feature is that it will make more men want to hold office, and once a man wants to hold a public office he is absolutely no good for honest work.

I thought I was going to have some farm relief to report to you by this day. But the commissions are just gathering data. They won't take the farmer's word for it that he is poor. They hire men to find out how poor he is. If they took all the money they spend on finding out how poor he is, and give it to the farmers he wouldn't need any more relief.

Postscript—Farmers get [some] relief today. Tariff was raised on window panes. Cheap glass from Glasgow has always hurt our agrarian glass growers.

You can't believe a thing you read in regard to officials' statements. The minute anything happens connected with official life, it's just like a cold night, everybody is trying to cover up.

You know I have often said in answer to inquiries as to how I got away with kidding some of our public men, that it was because I liked all of them personally, and that if there was no malice in your heart there could be none in your "gags," and I have always said I never met a man I didn't like.

Politicians can do more funny things naturally than I can think of to do purposely.

We have the best Congress money can buy.

On American Foreign Policy

The big nations would like to stick together. They say it's to protect the little ones, but it's to protect themselves. There is no nation lying awake at night worrying about a little nation unless that little nation is one where somebody can march across to get to them. Brotherly love has never crossed a boundary line yet. Yes, sir, geography has more to do with brotherly love than civilization and Christianity combined.

No nation has a monopoly on good things. Each one has something that the others could well afford to adopt.

Several papers have asked, "What would Europe do if we were in difficulties and needed help?"

So this is in reply to those inquiries: Europe would hold a celebration.

There's one thing no nation can accuse us of—that is secret diplomacy. Our foreign dealings are an open book—generally a check book.

We could never understand why Mexico wasn't just crazy about us; for we had always had their good will, and oil and coffee and minerals, at heart.

You take diplomacy out of war and the thing would fall flat in a week.

On Russia and Communism

It just looks to me like Communism is such a happy family affair that not a Communist wants to stay where it is practiced. It's the only thing they want you to have but keep none themselves.

Russia under the Czar was very little different from what it is today; for instead of one Czar, why, there is at least a thousand now. Any of the big men in the Party holds practically Czar-istic powers (to those down). Siberia is still work-ing. It's just as cold on you to be sent there un-der the Soviets as it was under the Czar.

Nobody knows what the outcome in Russia will be or how long this government will last. But if they do get by on everything else, they picked the only one thing I know of to suppress that is absolutely essential to run a country on, and that is religion. Never mind what kind, but it's got to be something or you will fail at the finish.

Communism is like Prohibition, it's a good idea but it won't work.

Travel Abroad

I see the customs authorities in England searched the round-the-world fliers when they landed. I guess they thought the boys had smuggled over a couple of baby grand pianos. . . . I was there last summer when Gertrude Ederle swam in from France [across the English Channel] and they searched her. Figured she had brought in some cigars or cigarettes or millinery in the

Flying was one of Will's favorite pastimes.

pockets of her bathing suit, I reckon. People tell you England has no humor. Why, they are funny even when they don't try to be.

I am going to keep flying up and down this Danube River till I find a place where it's blue.

A bunch of American tourists were hissed and stoned yesterday in France, but not until they had finished buying.

[France] is not a government; it's an old-fashioned movie, where they flash on the screen, "Two minutes, please, while we change Premiers."

I must tell you about Venice. I stepped out on the wrong side of a Venice taxicab . . . and they were three minutes fishing me out.

Rome has more churches and less preaching in them than any city in the world. Everybody wants to see where Saint Peter was buried, but nobody wants to try to live like him. . . .

Then another thing, I didn't know before I got there, and they told me all this, that Rome had Senators. Now I know why it declined.

We call Rome the seat of Culture—but somebody stole the chair. . . . If a town has any culture and tourists commence hitting it, your culture is gone. Tourists will rub it out of any town.

Cairo's a great place. I was the only tourist there who never went to see the Sphinx. I've seen Cal Coolidge.

Hawaii is the only place I know where they lay flowers on you while you are alive.

On Automobiles

Trouble with American transportation is that you can get somewhere quicker than you can think of a reason for going there. What we need now is a new excuse to go somewhere.

One way to solve the traffic problem would be to keep all the cars that are not paid for off the streets. Children could use the streets for playgrounds then.

The trouble with us is America is just muscle bound from holding a steering wheel; the only place we are callused from work is the bottom of our driving toe.

We have killed more people celebrating our Independence Day than we lost fighting for it.

Our automobiles don't stay at home long enough to know where homes are even if they could get back.

A lot of guys have had a lot of fun joking about Henry Ford because he admitted one time that he didn't know history. He don't know it, but history will know him. He has made more history than his critics has ever read.

On Clubs and Dinners

Two nuts can't go out to lunch together three times without one of them saying, "Let's form a club." Three men can't meet nowadays without one getting a gavel and the other two drawing up a constitution and by-laws.

I am going to be the founder of one club that is one with a purpose. Our purpose shall be to take a dying oath to murder every club member

Long-time friends Henry Ford and Will Rogers.

we meet. Then when we have thoroughly killed off every club member and there is no other club members left, to commit suicide ourselves and give the world a new start.

It is being "clubbed" to death.

If all the time consumed in attending dinners and luncheons was consumed in some work, the production of this country would be doubled.

Everybody is always belonging to some kind of a club today. Some people belong to everything but their own family.

Of Things Religious

The Lord put all these millions of people over the earth. They don't all agree on how they got here and ninety per cent don't care. But He was pretty wise when He did see to it that they all agree on one thing . . . and that is the better lives you live the better you will finish. No great religious revival will ever be started from an argument over where we come from. The religious revival of the future, when it comes, if started, will be people's fear over where they are going.

When I die, my epitaph or whatever you call those signs on gravestones is going to read: "I joked about every prominent man of my time, but I never met a man I didn't like." I am so proud of that I can hardly wait to die so it can be carved. And when you come to my grave you will find me sitting there, proudly reading it.

Of course, we are all just hanging on here as long as we can. I don't know why we hate to go, we know it's better there. Maybe it's because we haven't done anything that will live after we are gone.

If you live right, death is a joke to you as far as fear is concerned.

Why is it the good ones are the ones that go? That's one thing about an onery guy, you never hear of him dying. He is into everything else but a coffin.

Our religious beliefs are many, but one belief is universal with all, and that is that there is some divine being higher than earthly. We can speak to Him in many devious ways, in many languages, but He sees us all in the same light, and judges us according to our actions, as we judge the actions of our children different because we know they are each different.

Will had a number of comments during the famous Scopes "Monkey" Trial in Tennessee: Church people all over the country are divided and arguing over where we come from, neighbor. Women living next door to you will find out where you come from, and all about you, better than all the preachers. Just let the preachers make it their business where you are going when you leave here.

Believe in something for another world, but don't be too set on what it is, and then you won't start out that life with a disappointment. Live your life so that whenever you lose you are ahead.

On Education

It's funny how quick a college boy can find out that the world is wrong. He might go out in the world from high school and live in it, and make a living in it for years and think it wasn't such a bad place, but let him go to college and he will be the first one down on the square on May Day to shout down with the government.

But as soon as they grow up and go out and if they happen to make anything, why, they backslide.

The football season is about over. Education never had a more financial year. School will start now.

Successful colleges will start laying plans for a new stadium; unsuccessful ones will start hunting a new coach. . . .

There are more students in Columbia University than there are in any other in the world. . . . It is remarkable to have thirty-two hundred courses there. You spend the first two years in deciding what courses to take, the next two years in finding the building that these are given in, and the rest of your life in wishing you had taken another course.

They say children in kindergarten must play in order to get 'em to learn. What do you mean children? Crossword puzzles learned grown folks more words than school teachers. And what arithmetic the women folks know they

got at a bridge table. Our splendid English comes from attending the movies. My geography comes from an airplane window. Yes, sir, there is 120 million in the American kindergarten.

You know horses are smarter than people. You never heard of a horse going broke betting on people.

We got the most thorough training in every line of business but statesmanship, and for that you just decide overnight, "I'm a statesman."

Villains are getting as thick as college degrees and sometimes on the same fellow.

On Lawyers

If it weren't for wills, lawyers would have to work at an essential employment. There is only one way you can beat a lawyer in a death case. That is to die with nothing. Then you can't get a lawyer within ten miles of your house.

Modern history has proven that there has never yet been a will left that was carried out exactly as the maker of the money intended. So if you are thinking of dying and have money, I would advise you to leave the following will:

"Count up the lawyers in the state and divide it among them. If there should by any miracle be any left, let my relatives, all of them, God bless'em, fight over it."

Went down and spoke at some lawyers' meeting last night. They didn't think much of my little squib about driving the shysters out of their profession. They seemed to . . . doubt just who would have to leave.

I have always noticed that anytime a man can't come and settle with you without bringing his lawyer, why look out for him.

We are always saying, "Let the law take its course." But what we mean is "Let the law take *our* course."

The minute you read something and you can't understand it, you can *almost* be sure that it was drawn up by a lawyer. Then if you give it to another lawyer and he don't know just what it means, why then you *can* be sure it was drawn up by a lawyer. If it's in a few words and is plain

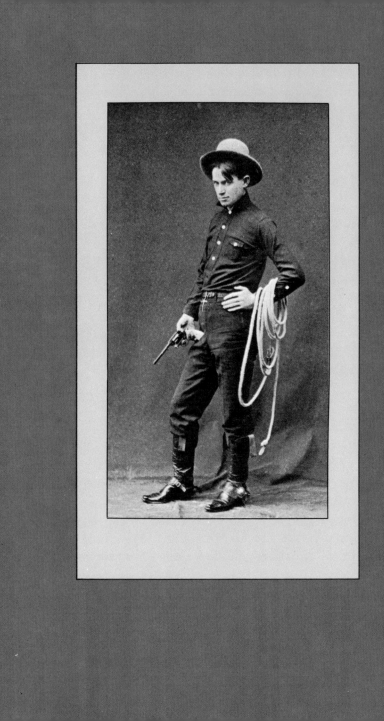

and understandable only one way, it was written by a non-lawyer.

The Movies

In 1934, Will was Master of Ceremonies at the "Oscar" presentations of the Academy of Motion Picture Arts and Sciences: This is the highest sounding named organization I ever attended. If I didn't know so many of the people who belonged to it personally I would have taken that name serious. . . .

There is great acting in this room tonight, greater than you will see on the screen. We all cheer when somebody gets a prize that everyone of us in the house knows should be ours. Yet we smile and take it. Boy, that's acting!

The average life of the movie is till it reaches the critic.

The average life of the movie hero is till he is found out.

Moving picture audiences are just like an old gold miner, they will keep on going and going

Will Rogers as he performed in wild west shows.   *49*

for years hoping against hope to someday strike a picture.

[Hollywood] will film the Lord's Supper and when it is made, figure out that it is not a good release title and not catchy enough, so it will be released under the heading, "A Red Hot Meal," or "The Gastronomical Orgy."

On Banks and The Stock Exchange

The banker, the lawyer, and the politician are still our best bets for a laugh. Audiences haven't changed at all, and neither has the three above professions.

If you think we are not prosperous and cuckoo both, read this: "Three hundred thousand dollars for seat on Stock Exchange." You pay that for a seat where nobody sits down. They stand and yell and sell something they haven't got, and buy something they will never get. . . . We must appear odd to the foreigners.

An old country boy banker from Colorado slicked the city-slicker bankers out of one-half million bucks and they give him fifteen years so fast that you would have thought he had assassinated a big government official. You let a city bank slick an old country boy out of something and before night it will merge with another bank and finally wind up as a member of the Federal Reserve.

Banking and after-dinner speaking are two of the most non-essential industries we have in this country, and I am willing to reform if they are.

On Newspapers

The newspaper women of all the papers formed a Newspaper Woman's Club and they give a big ball and I was asked to announce the acts. You know, women are doing all the writing on newspapers and magazines now. . . .

We had there women writers that cover everything. It would have been the greatest place in the world for some woman to have shot her husband. There were women murder writers that can tell from the smoke the caliber pistol used. Then there were the fashion editors that could have described her chemise frock while she did the shooting. Then the sob sister squad who could have almost made you feel sorry she only had one husband to shoot. Then, in case some man should have felt at home and wanted to knock his wife down, why the heart interest writers would have been on the job. So you see us people in public life want to stand in with those girls as we never know what might happen.

The funnies occupy four pages of the paper and editorials two columns. That proves that merit will tell.

Health and Doctors

Woman died at Savannah, Georgia, age 123. She had smoked a pipe for 112 years, while cigarette smokers figure they are passing out daily at the ripe old age of thirty and forty. I think it's the fatigue from tapping 'em on the cigarette case that wears 'em down so early.

This is a day of specializing, especially with the doctors. Say, for instance, there is something the

matter with your right eye. You go to a doctor and he tells you, "I am sorry, but I am a left-eye doctor; I make a specialty of left eyes." Take the throat business. A doctor that doctors on the upper part of your throat doesn't even know where the lower part goes to. . . .

The old-fashioned doctor didn't pick out a big toe or a left ear to make a life's living on. He picked the whole human frame. . . . Personally, I have always felt that the best doctor in the world is the veterinarian. He can't ask his patients what is the matter—he's got to just know.

Living in the Big Cities

Just passed thru Chicago. The snow was so deep today the crooks could only hit a tall man.

To try and diminish crime they laid off six hundred cops.

New Yorkers know nothing about the sun. The moon and sun mean nothing to a New Yorker. You can't see the sun out of the subway and you can't see the moon through the top of a taxicab. So when the two passed in eclipse [recently] it meant nothing in their lives.

New Yorkers were so used to traffic stops that they could not realize how any two objects could pass peacefully by each other without hitting. It was also the only thing ever took place back here that went off on schedule time.

I was in Chicago a few years ago during a janitor's strike. I never knew how you can tell when a janitor is on strike and when he ain't.

On War and Peace

I have a scheme for stopping war. It's this—no nation is allowed to enter a war till they have paid for the last one.

If we can just let other people alone and do their own fighting, we would be in good shape. When you get into trouble five thousand miles away from home you've got to have been looking for it.

There is only one way in the world to prevent war, and that is, FOR EVERY NATION TO TEND TO ITS OWN BUSINESS.

Trace any war that ever was and you will find

some nation was trying to tell some other nation how to run their business.

What degree of egotism is it that makes a nation or a religious organization think theirs is the very thing for the Chinese or the Zulus? Why, we can even Christianize our legislators.

On Truth and Talk

Discontent comes in proportion to knowledge. The more you know the more you realize you don't know.

People's minds are changed through observation and not through argument.

Everybody is ignorant, only on different subjects.

When ignorance gets started it knows no bounds.

I don't know opera but I know common sense and the commoner the better I know it.

More words ain't good for anything in the world only to bring on more argument.

Nobody wants his cause near as bad as he wants to talk about his cause.

We do more talking progress than we do progressing.

Liberty don't work near as good in practice as it does in speeches.

Rumor travels faster, but it don't stay put as long as truth.

A remark generally hurts in proportion to its truth.

Philosophical Thoughts

What constitutes a life well spent? Love and admiration from our fellow men is all that anyone can ask.

Everyone of us in the world have our audience to play to; we study them and we try to do it so it will appeal to what we think is the great majority. We all have our particular little line of applesauce for each occasion. So let's be honest with ourselves, and not take ourselves too seri-ous, and never condemn the other fellow for doing what we are doing every day, only in a different way.

This thing of being a hero, about the main thing to it is to know when to die. Prolonged life has ruined more men than it ever made.

Popularity is the easiest thing in the world to gain and it is the hardest thing to hold.

Everyone has deep in their heart the old town or community where they first went barefooted, got their first licking, traded the first pocket knife, grew up and finally went away thinking they were too big for that Burg. But that's where your old heart is.

You got to sorter give and take in this old world. We can get mighty rich, but if we haven't got any friends, we will find we are poorer than anybody.

Heroes are made every little while, but only one in a million conduct themselves afterwards so that it makes us proud that we honored them at the time.

It's only the inspiration of those who die that makes those who live realize what constitutes a useful life.

It's great to be great, but it's greater to be human.

We may elevate ourselves but we should never reach so high that we would ever forget those who helped us get there.

We will never have true civilization until we have learned to recognize the rights of others.

Everybody has got a scheme to get the world right again. I can't remember when it was ever right. There has been times when it was right for you and you and you, but never all at the same time. The whole thing is a teeter-board even when it's supposed to be going good. You are going up and somebody is coming down. You can't make a dollar without taking it from somebody. So everytime you wish for something for your own personal gain, you are wishing somebody else bad luck, so maybe that's why so few of our wishes come to anything.

You must judge a man's greatness by how much he will be missed.

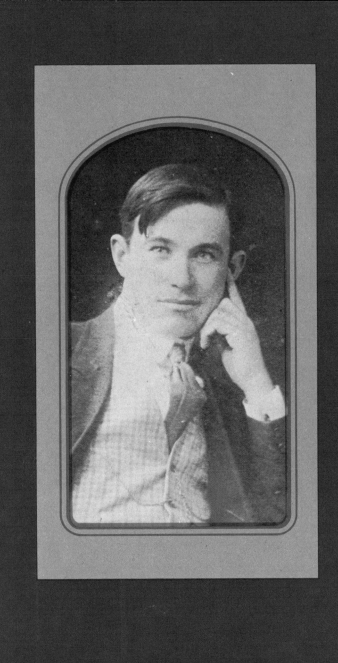

Important Dates in Will Rogers' Life

1879 Born November 4 near Claremore, Oklahoma (then Indian Territory), the eighth child of Clem and Mary Rogers.

1898 Left school for the last of many times to work as a cowboy in Texas.

1902 Went to South Africa in Texas Jack's Wild West Show, then to Australia and New Zealand with the Wirth Bros. Circus.

1904 First vaudeville bookings in Chicago.

1908 Married to Betty Blake on November 25.

1916 Began nine-year association with the Ziegfeld *Follies*.

1918 Starred in the first of his seventy movies, "Laughing Bill Hyde."

1919 Published his first writings in two small books. Moved to California.

1922 Began his syndicated newspaper articles,
        which he continued the rest of his life.
        Also made his first radio broadcast.

1926 Appointed Mayor of Beverly Hills.

1927 First civilian to fly from coast to coast
        with mail pilots.

1935 Killed on August 15 at age 55 in an
        airplane crash near Point Barrow, Alaska,
        with Wiley Post, famous flier.

The five Rogers in Long Island, New York.